Busting Addiction Wide Open from a Biblical Perspective

Hello My Name Is....

Copper B.

Hello, My Name Is…

Book Cover Design by ebooklaunch.com
ISBN 979-8-391-688266

Other Titles By the Author

Broken to Beautiful: Trusting in God to Heal and Restore a Life Spent Hiding Behind an Addict

Broken Boy Mended Man: How to Overcome Rejection and Abandonment through the Healing Love of Jesus

Contents

"Then you will know the truth,
and the truth will set you free."

John 8:32

Disclaimer

This book is not intended to provide medical expertise or psychological diagnosis concerning any type of addiction or habit forming behaviors. Neither is it a substitute for your decision or lack thereof to seek additional sound Biblical Counseling when needed or prompt medical attention in the event that a serious situation arises. The writings in this book are my opinions and belief based on my knowledge and comprehension of God's Word as shown to me by the Holy Spirit. In addition, our desire as a ministry and representation of Jesus Christ is not to be in discordance with any organization, medical practitioner or church. However, our purpose IS to motivate the reader to seek the Holy Spirit and search the truths in God's Word for THEMSELVES. Our burning passion is to see others set free through the Power of the Holy Spirit in Jesus Name. This book is designed to impart the belief that Jesus/ the Holy Spirit/ God's Word alone is sufficient enough to deliver you from any addiction you may face and ultimately transform your life.

Preface

I spent many hours in conversation with the Holy Spirit seeking God's guidance on exactly what to cover in the pages of this book. Addiction in many forms has impacted both mine and my husband's lives in one way or another. It incapacitated my personal life for decades while I helplessly hid within the shadows. I perished slowly behind closed doors where the secrets of substance abuse thrived in darkness. Back then, I did not understand my authority in Christ nor have the spiritual knowledge I now contain. Through our past experiences surrounding addiction in many forms God birthed our ministry, Mended Heart. In our travels we began to discover addiction in some form was spreading rampantly everywhere in society. No matter how hard people tried to recover they seemed to always still be recovering from one thing or another. As we grew in our relationship with the Lord and began to experience the Power of the Holy Spirit in our lives the scales started to fall off. We arrived at the realization that addictions; whether they be alcohol, drugs, codependency, food disorders and so on are actually spirits attached to misdirected pain which opened the door for demonic influence in the first place. The reason people are continually recovering is because they never gain true freedom. The more I began to write, the more insight began to flow. I remember having a conversation with the Holy Spirit and questioning whether or not everything I was writing was an overload of information. The response from the Lord was always the same: "give them meat." In turn, the goal of this book is to do just that. Move you beyond the surface of the Bible with your natural vision and take you into the meat of God's Word through spiritual eyes. Our aim is to provide you with an in depth understanding of the actuality of addiction by supplying you with sound knowledge rooted in the truths of Scripture. In addition, to supply you with the spiritual insight necessary to discern the source behind your addictive behaviors and enable you to heal those wounds. Most importantly, to help you comprehend your undisputed Christ identity, confirm the strength of your AUTHORITY through Christ Jesus, and cling to the Power of the Holy Spirit in order to obtain true freedom.

What Is It?

Anyone can clearly see the physical suffering addiction causes and the torment it brings to the soul (mind and emotions.) The world will tell you addiction is a disease. It is characterized as an illness that can be managed, but never really cured. The Church on the other hand will tell you it is just sin. In order to see fundamental change and freedom from addictive behaviors you must begin to understand the source behind it. True addiction originates in the spiritual realm and is authored by satan. At its core it is spiritual in nature, but the root source of all addiction is not just sin, neither is it a disease as a result of sin. It is an evil spirit. A

True addiction originates in the spiritual realm and is authored by satan.

demon attached to the sin that takes control of your mind and emotions. The physical part of addiction that affects the chemical biology of the brain is just an outward manifestation of the demon on the inside.

The physical part of addiction that affects the chemical biology of the brain is just an outward manifestation of the demon on the inside

When you do not recognize that addiction is actually being influenced by a spiritual force then you are more willing to label it as merely a physical or emotional problem and thus limit the actual cure.

As uncomfortable as the reality of an attested demonic realm may sound God's Word discusses this type of activity is taking place.

For our struggle is not against flesh and blood, but against rulers, against authorities, against the powers of this dark world and against the spiritual forces of evil in the heavenly realms. Ephesians 6:12 NIV

Addiction is initially created from pain, trauma, generational curses, feelings of shame, fear, anger, sadness, and the list goes on and on. Children are especially vulnerable because they have no coping skills and many times no one to help them navigate their pain God's way. In consequence, whether it be a child or an adult deep pain creates a wound. A place within the soul that holds all that torment and heartache in an effort to shield and protect. When that wound is not dealt with and healed a spiritual door is opened. A door that allows an evil spirit to come in and sit on top of that wound causing affliction and addiction. In essence, the soul is sick and, therefore, under attack.

When people who suffer with addiction initially experience pain and trauma they knowingly or unknowingly look to the world to fill that pain. Whether that be in the form of codependency, anger, fear, drugs, alcohol, work, sex, repetitive buying, binge eating or other addictive behavior patterns used to fill a void. It is an empty spot or area where they don't feel adequate, loved or needed.

When people who suffer with addiction initially experience pain and trauma they knowingly or unknowiingly look to the world to fill that pain

Do you know it is not wrong to long and desire something all of the time. God created your heart with a habitual yearning and a thirst. He wants you to long for Him because it is in that longing that you are fulfilled by God.

> In order to understand what addiction is at its root you must confirm who you are in Christ Jesus

He has made everything beautiful and appropriate in its time. He has also planted eternity (a sense of divine purpose) in the human heart (a mysterious longing which nothing under the sun can satisfy, except God), yet man cannot find out (comprehend, grasp) what God has done (His overall plan) from the beginning to the end. Ecclesiastes 3:11 AMP

> He wants you to long for Him because it is in that longing that you are fulfilled by God

It is only when you look to the world to drive out pain that you are filled with an empty hope of false gratification. A gratification built on the shallow foundation of who you believed yourself to be. That lie of satan is what stands in direct opposition to the truth God has provided in His Word establishing who you are and who He, God, created you to be. In order to understand what addiction is at its root you must first denounce that lie and confirm who you are in Christ Jesus.

Who Am I?

We travel many places in ministry praying over, counseling, and ministering to countless individuals consumed inside the battle of addiction. Once we start to connect with people and delve into their past we begin to see a pattern. Regardless, if the person is saved by the blood of Jesus or does not yet know Him ALL have one thing in common. They do not know their Christ identity. The same applies to you. If you are struggling with addictive behaviors you have not fully learned who you are in Christ, who He made you to be, or your God given purpose.

Addiction is birthed when you do not know who you are in Christ

Addiction is birthed when you do not know who you are in Christ. From the moment you were born this world began to compare you to others. Not to mention some of you were born directly into homes of rejection and abandonment, pain or trauma. Others while still in the womb. In consequence, you began to think, "I am not enough." Right from the very beginning you started to believe the lies of the devil and your identity was misplaced. You sought out who and what your value was everywhere but in the one place that mattered. God. The Creator Himself.

Right from the very beginning you started to believe the lies of the devil and your identity was misplaced

Go back to the very beginning of creation to see your worth and identity.

What does God say?

His Word says...

We are created in "His image."

So God created human beings in His own image.

In the image of God He created them; male and female He created them. Genesis 1:27 NKJV

God is more than a phsyical being

God is a spirit, and those who worship Him must worship Him in spirit and truth. John 4:24 NKJV

God is more than a physical being. He is not confined to seeing or hearing or being in one location. The fact that we are created in "the image" of God means we are spiritual in being just as He is.

But, we are human, right?

Flesh and bone.

Here is where it gets hard to comprehend, but necessary to understand. We are indeed human. God created us out of the dust of the earth. We have a human body.

Then the Lord God formed man out of the dust from the ground and breathed the breath of life into his nostrils, and the man became a living being. Genesis 2:7 NIV

But because we are created in God's image we are also a spirit. God is a spiritual being. He does not have a human form. He is the Holy Spirit. Hence, the Trinity: God the Father, God the Son, and God the Holy Spirit. They are three in one. Three separate beings with different functions, yet still One. One God. One being.

> Because we are created in God's image we are also a spirit

Being human makes this concept extremely difficult to comprehend. Our mind can't fathom it.

In addition to that, many Christians and the church as a whole have confused this concept in God's Word. We are taught from a very young age that our soul and spirit are the same thing. That we have a soul and a body. The soul being the part that can choose Jesus and go to heaven when you die, and the body which is just an outer shell that returns to the dust of the ground.

Then the dust will return to the earth as it was, And the spirit will return to God who gave it. Ecclesiastes 12:7 NKJV

You are more than just a soul and a body. You are, in fact, a three part being.

Contemplate that for a moment.

God is a three part being is He not?

Do you remember the Trinity?

He is God the Father, God the Son and God the Holy Spirit.

> You are a spirit that lives in a body and has a soul

So, if we are created in God's image like scripture states, would it not make sense that we too are also a three part being?

Look at it this way.

You are a spirit that lives in a body and has a soul.

Read that again.

YOU ARE A SPIRIT THAT LIVES IN A BODY AND HAS A SOUL.

Let's break that down for a moment.

Your spirit is where God, the Holy Spirit resides inside of you. Your spirit represents the Holy Spirit.

> It is God's breath that came in you and made you alive

It is God's breath that came in you and made you alive.

Then the LORD God formed a man from the dust of the ground and breathed into his nostrils the breath of life, and the man became a living being. Genesis 2:7 NIV

Your spirit is what gets born again.

Picture that every baby is born with their own spirit that is dead/dormant if you will. The only way that spirit comes alive is when you accept Jesus. Your SPIRIT is what gets born again. Not your body and not your soul.

Your soul is your mind, will, and emotions. The place inside you that holds all your feelings.

People confuse these as one object/entity and therefore just interchange the two. However, the spirit and soul are different. They are not the same.

His Word Says…

For the word of God is alive and active. Sharper than any double-edged sword, it penetrates even to dividing soul and spirit, joints and marrow; it judges the thoughts and attitudes of the heart. Hebrews 4:12 NIV

If something can be separated/divided then they are two different things.

This is also why the Bible says to renew your mind(soul) and crucify the flesh (body).

When you agree with sin Satan can enter your mind and afflict your body

It is an ongoing process that continues until the day you die. That is called sanctification.

Your body is your flesh and blood. It most represents Jesus because He came to earth in His fleshly form.

Your body, that earthly part of you is where satan can harass, tempt and torment because of the sin you have let into your life. When you agree with sin satan and his demons can enter your mind and emotions and afflict your body.

When you grasp that truth you can begin to recognize how and where addiction creeps in and starts to take hold.

Many argue unbelievers are the only ones that can have demons. The argument is based on the belief that if you have demons you are demon possessed.

His Word Says…

"And you know that God anointed Jesus of Nazareth with the Holy Spirit and with power. Then Jesus went around doing good and healing all who were oppressed by the devil, for God was with him." Acts 10:38 NLT

Having the Holy Spirit does not prevent you from having demons

Peter did not say in this passage Jesus went around healing the demon possessed. He said Jesus went around healing the demon oppressed. People under the control of demonic oppression.

What is oppression then?

Oppression is simply an abuse of power or authority over a life.

So, who gives the devil authority to come in and beat you down?

You do!

God gives you a choice whether or not to serve Him even after you are born again.

That is the key phrase.

YOU HAVE A CHOICE.

Having the Holy Spirit does not prevent you from having demons.

You still have control over what you do with your body, mind and emotions.

The Holy Spirit convicts you as a believer. He does not control you.

His Word Says…

The Holy Spirit convicts you as a believer, he does not control you

"Do you not know that you are the temple of God and that the Spirit of God dwells in you? If anyone defiles the temple of God, God will destroy him. For the temple of God is holy, which temple you are." I Corinthians 3:16-17 ESV

Even as a believer you can have demons when you open the doors to sin. They can coexist within your flesh. This does not mean demons reside in communion where the Holy Spirit is.

The Holy Spirit lives inside of you. He doesn't commune with demonic spirits. He can, however, coexist with them in the same way He coexists with your flesh.

You are a spirit and the Holy Spirit lives IN you, but NOT in your body

You are a spirit and the Holy Spirit lives IN you, but NOT in your body.

Having the Holy Spirit does not mean that other ungodly influences cannot operate in you as a result of your choice to engage in sin. What it does mean is that they cannot own you.

There is not one verse in scripture that mirrors the belief that if a person has a demon they cannot have God. As a believer you STILL belong to God.

As a believer you still belong to God

"My Father, who has given them to Me, is greater than all, and no one is able to snatch them out of the Father's Hand." John 10:29 ESV

This is why it is so important to develop a solid foundation and understanding of who you are in Christ. When you know what is declared in scripture then you are less apt to doubt yourself. God is the answer to your identity. It's not about who you are. It's really all about who HE is.

It's not about who you are. It's really all about who HE is.

God is eternal. The beginning (Alpha) and the end (Omega) and everything in between. Even before the world was formed God existed. He created everything because He is Almighty. No enemy can defeat Him. He destroys them with just the breath of His mouth.

The man of lawlessness (antichrist) will be revealed, but the Lord Jesus will kill him with the breath of His mouth and destroy him by the splendor of His coming. 2 Thessalonians 2:8 NLT

Do not doubt for one minute that God can't do for you what you could never do for yourself.

"I am the Alpha and the Omega," says the Lord God, "Who is and Who was and Who is to come, the Almighty." Revelation 1:8 NKJV

He is everywhere, anywhere, and nowhere

Never question He does not see you or care about your anguish. He is everywhere, anywhere, and nowhere.

When God instructed Moses to lead the Jewish people (Israel) out of slavery from Egypt. Moses responded with doubt and objection. However, God answered him with the promise of HIS own presence by saying, "I will be with You."

God is with you

So He said, "I will certainly be with you. And this shall be a sign to you that I have sent you: When you have brought the people out of Egypt, you shall serve God on this mountain." Exodus 3:12 NKJV

That is God's answer to you as well.
In all things.
At all times.
He is with you.

Every feeling of I'm not good enough, every painful circumstance, every failure you have ever experienced. God is there with His limitless resources. You just have to ask.

"Call to Me and I will answer you, and tell you (and even show you) great and mighty things, (things which have been confined and hidden), which you do not know and understand and cannot distinguish." James 33:3 AMP

When you do not know your identity or purpose in Christ you begin to look for love in all the wrong places

His Word Says ...

For we are God's masterpiece. He has created us anew in Christ Jesus, so we can do the good things He planned for us long ago. Ephesians 2:10 NLT

We are created for a purpose.

You are unique and have your very own God given purpose.

When you do not know your identity or purpose in Christ you begin to look for love in all the wrong places.

The number one need as a human is love

Why?

The number one need as a human is love.

Do you know that is why God sent His Son Jesus?

He is the ultimate love sacrifice. He conquered sin and death on the cross and that included addiction. Nothing, NOTHING can separate you from His unconditional love.

His Word Says...

For I am persuaded, that neither death, nor life, nor angels, nor principalities, nor powers, nor things present, nor things to come, nor height, nor depth, nor any other creature, shall be able to separate us from the love of God, which is in Christ Jesus our Lord. Romans 8:38-39 NKJV

Our primary attachment should be God. When it is not it is inevitable you will become attached to something else.

> You are not of this world

When you do not know who you are in Christ and that God loves you – GOD loves YOU, that is when you start to look to the world for release from pain. You place your identity on whether or not others think you are worth their time, attention or love. You let your sense of identity be defined by this fallen world and other broken and damaged people. These sources sooner or later crumble and fall apart. But God says we are not of this world.

We are to be set apart.

"If you belonged to the world, it would love you as its own. As it is, you do not belong to the world, but I have chosen you out of the world. That is why the world hates you. John 15:19 NIV

> The devil will always whisper lies about your identitiy. You must break the power of those lies by declaring your identity in Christ

The character and purpose of God is

redemptive in nature. They are to bring life. You have to begin to understand God and allow Him to define who you are.

The devil will always whisper lies to you about your identity. You must break the power of those lies by declaring your identity in Christ.

Say OUTLOUD....
I am a child of God.
I am healed.
I am forgiven.
I am righteous.
God says,...
Renounce yourself.
Empty yourself.
Fill yourself with God,
and Come follow Me.

Then He called the crowd to Him along with His disciples and said: "Whoever wants to be My disciple must deny themselves and take up their cross and follow Me. " Mark 8:34 NIV

You must first choose to follow Christ.

But seek first His Kingdom and his righteousness, and all these things will be given to you as well. Matthew 6:33 NIV

For God so loved the world that He gave His only begotten Son, that whosoever believeth in Him should not perish but have everlasting life. John 3:16 KJV

in your relationship with Christ is where you will find Him, and thus your identity

Begin to have a relationship with HIM.

In your relationship with Christ is where you will find Him, and thus your identity. By finding your own identity in Christ you will be able to obtain true freedom from your addictions.

"For I know the plans I have for you," declares the Lords, "plans to prosper you and not to harm you, plans to give you hope and a future.

Then you will call on Me and come and pray to Me, and I will listen to you.

You will seek Me and find Me when you seek Me with all your heart. Jeremiah 29:11-13 NIV

When Will I Be Free?

You've managed to stay steady for a while. Those desperate urges have finally subsided to a quiet yet constant background noise. They occupy the hidden corners in the outskirts of your mind where you pretend they don't exist. You've learned to accept them as just a part of the aftermath. Subtle yet annoying reminders of who you once were and still are in many ways.

Some of you accepted Jesus as your Savior and stopped there. While others actually have a relationship with Him. You KNOW Him.

What does that mean?....

I can say I know Michael Jordan, but I don't really know him. I don't have a relationship with him that includes talking to him, seeing him, or knowing intimate things about him such as his family's likes or dislikes.

> You have to get rid of the spirit operating behind the addiction

The same is true for anyone struggling with addictions. If you want to truly be free from addictive behaviors you have to ground yourself in the One who makes a way. Stay in God's Word and imprint it in your heart, mind, and soul.

I have hidden Your Word in my heart that I might not sin against You. Psalm 119:11 NIV

Memorize it.

Most importantly, you have to get rid of the spirit(s) that are operating behind the addiction.

As long as they remain they will have the ability to harass you. You can change habits, work on breaking patterns and go to rehab. You can even attend the recovery program at your church. Most will tell you recovery is a continuous process.

Yes, recovery is a process, but it doesn't have to last forever.

Have you ever said to yourself, Why can't I get free?

Have you ever wondered why before and after a recovery meeting you see people outside smoking cigarettes or vaping?

Treating the symptoms of demonic strongholds or managing a "disease" does not bring true freedom

Many would argue that smoking cigarettes or getting multiple tattoos is less destructive than shooting cocaine or binge eating until you gain one hundred pounds. Treating the symptoms of demonic strongholds or managing a "disease" does not bring true freedom. Just like cutting off a weed at the ground does not kill it. It merely sets the stage for thicker, stronger regrowth in the future.

Demons do not want you to know they are there. They want to hide in the shadows. They like to piggyback on issues you already have instead of creating new problems.

Meanwhile, you thought you healed from your addiction. You dealt with your rejection and abandonment issues, pain, sorrow, anger, pride, hatred, despair and the list goes on and on.

In reality, all those demons were not recognized as what they were. Demons. In consequence, they stayed hidden and waiting until your next big catastrophe.

Do you find yourself doing the same thing over and over again. You are not able to control or stop the impulse. After you do it you feel tormented. You even ask yourself why. Why did I do that?

I was getting better.

You say you'll never do it again. But.....

That is not temptation of the flesh as many might believe. It is a spirit! It just wants you to believe the temptation is fleshly.

If the demon can convince you the behavior is part of an addictive pattern linked to your DNA and that pattern is what ultimately caused your

If the demon can convince you the behavior is part of an addictive pattern linked to your DNA and that pattern is what ultimately caused your "substance use disorder" then it has successfully fulfilled it's job "substance use disorder" then it has successfully fulfilled it's job. Staying hidden and undetected allows the demon to keep the lie of addiction going. If it can falsify the source it can keep you bound. One of the easiest ways satan accomplishes this is by using your own spoken words.

EVERY time you stand up in a group or say outloud, "I am a recovering addict."

Hi, my name is ________ and I am a ____________ or I "have" anger or anxiety or whatever.

You are declaring the addiction and affliction over yourself!

Do NOT call yourself an addict.

Do NOT say you have an addictive personality.

Do NOT confess the behavior as your addiction.

When you take ownership of your addiction such terminology is used and unknowingly you word curse yourself!

His Word Says…

The tongue can bring death or life; those who love to talk will reap the consequences. Proverbs 18:21 NLT

The soothing tongue is a tree of life, but a perverse tongue crushed the spirit. Proverbs 15:4 NIV

When you take ownership of your addiction such terminology is used and unkowingly you word curse yourself

Speaking rashly is like a piercing sword, but the tongue of the wise brings healing. Proverbs 12:18 BST

With the tongue we praise our Lord and Father, and with it we curse humans beings, who have been made in God's likeness. James 3:9 NLT

Words have power! They can build up or tear down. They bring life or death physically, emotionally and spiritually.

Jesus came so that you could choose life over death. All that anguish you are experiencing now. All that addiction Jesus took upon Himself and left at the cross. When He died for you it was healed. When He rose

Words have power

again on the third day victory became yours. Your freedom was sealed!

Don't let anybody tell you complete freedom from addiction is not achievable.

Don't let anybody tell you complete freedom from addiciton is not achievable

His Word Says…

"But He was wounded for our transgressions, He was bruised for our iniquities; The chastisement for our peace was upon Him, and BY HIS STRIPES WE ARE HEALED." Isaiah 53:5 NKJV

By His stripes we are healed. According to scripture Jesus was whipped and shed His blood so we could be healed in our spirit, soul, and body. When you spend time in God's Word you will begin to understand that the atonement of Jesus' Blood does in fact provide physical, spiritual, and emotional healing.

To be free from addiction you need to be delivered by the power of the Blood of Jesus. When He died on the cross that included deliverance from demonic forces that come to steal your freedom.

> To be free from addiction you need to be delivered by the power of the blood of Jesus

The thief (satan) comes only to steal and kill and destroy; I have come that they may have life, and have it to the full. John 10:10 NIV

The battle against addiction cannot be waged using human techniques. It requires spiritual weapons.

For though we live in the world, we do not wage war as the world does.

The weapons we fight with are not the weapons of the world. On the contrary, they have divine power to demolish strongholds. 2 Corinthians 10:3-4 NIV

> The battle against addiction cannot be waged using human techniques.

The HOLY SPIRIT is our weapon against addiction, and true believers have full access to His power.

When you receive Christ as your Savior the Holy Spirit enters into you.

It is the HOLY SPIRIT who comes into your spirit when you accept Jesus.

It is the HOLY SPIRIT who goes everywhere with you.

It is the HOLY SPIRIT who speaks, comforts and convicts you.

Salvation is all about the Holy Spirit entering in. The Bible also speaks about being infilled or baptized in the Holy Spirit. Many born again Christians believe when you accept Christ as your Savior that is also when you receive the Baptism of the Holy Spirit. I can affirm through scripture and personal experience these are two separate actions, and here is the difference:

Salvation is all about the Holy Spirit entering in

Salvation is to create/activate the life of God inside of you.

Baptism of the Holy Spirit is the empowerment with the gifts of the Holy Spirit through the Power of God.

Baptism of the Holy Spirit is the empowerment with the gifts of the Holy Spirit through the power of God

Not long after Jesus rose from the grave He showed Himself to the disciples.

Again Jesus said, "Peace be with you! As the Father has sent Me, I am sending you."

And with that He breathed on them and said, "Receive the Holy Spirit." John 20:21-22 NIV

When Phillip went to Samaria in Acts chapter 8 he preached the gospel to the people. They believed in the gospel of Jesus, became born again and were water baptized. However, see this.

They did NOT receive the baptism of the Holy Spirit until Peter and John came and prayed for them to receive Him.

The Holy Spirit had not yet come upon any of them, for they had only been baptized in the Name of the Lord Jesus (water baptism).

Then Peter and John laid their hands upon these believers, and they received the Holy Spirit. Acts 8:14-18 NLT

And again when Paul passed through Ephesus.

And he said to them, "Did you receive the Holy Spirit when you believed(got saved)?" And they said, "No, we have not even heard that there is a Holy Spirit." And he said, "Into what were you baptized?" They said, "Into John's baptism(water baptism)." And Paul said, "John baptized with the baptism of repentance, telling the people to believe in the One who was to come after Him, that is, Jesus." On hearing this, they were baptized in the Name of the Lord Jesus. And when Paul had laid hands on them, the Holy Spirit came on them, and they began speaking in tongues and prophesying. Acts 19:1-7 NKJV

All of these people received Christ as their Savior first and then later got baptized in the Holy Spirit.

It was NOT at the same time.

Before Jesus came to this earth as a human, He was also a spirit, just like God, His Father and the Holy Spirit. When Jesus went back to heaven He told his disciples the Holy Spirit would come in His place so He could be everywhere at once.

Jesus told His disciples to wait in Jerusalem for the promise of the Father.

And being assembled together with them, He commanded them not to depart from Jerusalem, but to wait for the promise of the Father, which He said, "you have heard from me; for John truly baptized with water, but you shall be baptized with the Holy Spirit not many days from now." Act 1:4-5 NKJV

"And now I will send the Holy Spirit, just as my Father promised. But stay here in the city until the Holy Spirit comes and fills you with power from heaven." Luke 24:49 NLT

How many of you have been baptized in water?

Being baptized in water is an outward expression to show others that you have decided to accept Jesus as your Savior and follow Him. When you enter the waters of baptism you are proclaiming you are dead to the power of sin and are now raised up in new life with Christ. You went down under the water until you were completely soaked, immersed right?

God wants us to be completely submerged, covered, and soaked in the Spirit of God

Symbolically, that is how being baptized in the Spirit is. God wants us to be completely submerged, covered, and soaked in the Spirit of God. No part of you will then be left untouched by His Spirit. When you are infilled with the Holy Spirit you will be able to experience an overflow of His presence and power. By yourself you cannot do much, but the Holy Spirit working through you can do mighty miracles. The Baptism of the Holy Spirit is all about Him flowing out. Out of you with His Power.

> The baptism of the Holy Spirit is all about Him flowing out

It is the HOLY SPIRIT who fills you with His Power.

But, you will receive power when the Holy Spirit has come upon you, and you will be My witnesses in Jerusalem and in all Judea and Samaria, and to the end of the earth." Acts 1:8 ESV

And it shall come to pass afterward that I will pour out My Spirit on all flesh; your sons and your daughters shall prophesy, your old men shall dream dreams, your young men shall see visions. And also on my menservants and on my maidservants I will pour out My Spirit in those days. Joel 2:28-29 NKJV

Addiction HAS to be conquered by the HOLY SPIRIT!

> Addiction has to be conquered by the Holy Spirit

If you want to beat your battle with addiction and win in ALL areas of addictive behavior you will need the power of the Holy Spirit flowing through you.

Jesus explained if you want to receive the indwelling of the Holy Spirit and be clothed in His Power all you have to do is ask. It's that simple.

Ask for the Holy Spirit and then believe you have received Him.

"If you then, being evil, know how to give good gifts to your children, how much more will your heavenly Father give the Holy Spirit to those who ask Him!" Luke 11:13 NKJV

"So I say to you, ask and it will be given to you; seek ,and you will find: knock, and it will be opened to you." Matthew 7:7 ESV

"For everyone who asks receives, and he who seeks finds, and to him who knocks it will be opened." Luke 11:10 NKJV

You don't have to be in a church service or in front of a preacher to receive the baptism of the Holy Spirit. You can receive Him anywhere.

In the quietness of the moment close your eyes and cry out for the Holy Spirit to come in His Power.

Heavenly Father, I come to you in Jesus Name. I ask you even now to fill me with Your Holy Spirit. Clothe me in Your Power, and baptize me with Your Holy Fire. According to the promises in Your Word, I believe that You will come, and that by faith I have received Your Holy Spirit into my life right now. Thank you gracious Father God in Jesus' Name. Amen.

For it is the power of the Holy Spirit that sets you free

Do not get in a hurry. Wait for His presence to fill where you are. Be patient. Keep praying and seeking. He will come.

Now it is time to live by the Power of the Holy Spirit. For it is the POWER of the HOLY SPIRIT that sets you free.

Now the Lord is the Spirit, and where the Spirit of the Lord is, there is freedom. 2 Corinthians 3:17 NIV

Where Does My Authority Come From?

While God's Power is displayed through the Holy Spirit, it is the Authority of Christ that allows us to use it. Authority as expressed in the ministries of Jesus and His disciples is the ability, power, or right to do something. We have been given authority in Christ as children of God, and according to Jesus we have been given the authority to cast out demons, heal the sick, and defeat the works of satan.

"Behold, I have given you AUTHORITY to tread on serpents and scorpions (demons), and over all the POWER of the enemy, and nothing shall hurt you. Luke 10:19 ESV

"Truly, truly I say unto you, whoever believes in Me will also do the works that I do, and greater works than these will he do, because I am going to the Father. John 14:12 ESV

If you want to be most effective at winning your battle against addiction you must go beyond simply believing to ACTING on the authority you have been given. It is your faith to display Jesus' Authority that will initiate the release of God's Power to carry out His Will. When you realize you are indeed fighting a spiritual battle where addiction is a demon you will be able to use the SAME Authority given to you by Jesus to obtain freedom.

If you want to be most effective at winning your battle against addiction you must go beyond simply believing to acting on the authority you have been given

Jesus said, "In My Name, you will cast out demons…" Mark 16:17 NIV

If you are a believer in Jesus then you are under HIS NAME. Therefore, this authority is given to you as a believer of Christ Jesus. You do not have to be a preacher or in ministry to cast out demons. Part of your assignment as a believer in Christ is to cast them out.

You are called by Jesus to do so. It is time for you to walk under His Authority.

"As you go, proclaim this message: The Kingdom of Heaven has come near. Heal the sick, raise the dead, cleanse those who have leprosy, drive out demons. Freely you have received; freely give." Matthew 10:7-8 NIV

If you fully grasp the authority given to you in Christ then the recovery process beyond your addiction will NOT last. If you are still declaring recovery from addictive behaviors or habits ten, fifteen or even thirty years after your initial deliverance from your main addiction, my friend, you never obtained true freedom in the beginning.

If you fully grasp the authority given to you in Christ then the recovery process beyond your addiction will not last

I am not stating that you will always have demons on the inside of you. I am not declaring that everyone has demons living within. However, we live in a fallen world, and satan and his minions will harass and torment your flesh(the outside) time and time again. You are human, and as long as you are alive here on this earth you will have your carnal nature to contend with.

Dearly beloved, I beseech you as strangers and pilgrims, abstain from fleshly lusts, which war against the soul. I Peter 2:11 KJV

When you allow your flesh to take over; you give it a place in your heart. In consequence, you will always have trouble in your soul. satan attacks your mind and emotions. When you don't resist the thoughts, yet instead yield to the flesh by conjuring up plans in order to fulfill your desires that is what gives him an open door.

When you allow your flesh to take over; you give it a place in your heart

THAT is what allows demons to enter in.

They have access through open doors.

THAT is how they operate,

And THAT is why your addictive behaviors never disappear completely.

This is where your authority comes into play. If an evil spirit is trying to work through your flesh , you have AUTHORITY OVER IT!

But, ONLY as long as you are walking in line with the Word of God and not falling prey to temptations of the flesh.

> Demons obey the authority of Jesus name

Demons obey the Authority of Jesus Name. That is why it is vital that you speak OUTLOUD and command them to leave IN THE NAME OF JESUS.

And these signs will accompany those who believe: "IN MY NAME they will drive out demons; they will speak in new tongues; they will pick up snakes with their hands; and when they drink deadly poison, it will not hurt them at all; they will place their hands on sick people, and they will get well."

After the Lord Jesus had spoken to them, He was taken up into heaven and He sat at the right hand of God. Then His disciples went out and preached everywhere, and the Lord worked with them and confirmed His Word by the signs that accompanied it. Mark 16:17-20 NIV

Do not convey through this scripture that Jesus is suggesting you pick up, handle, or throw around venomous and deadly snakes or physically drink poison. When reading God's Word you must begin to allow the Holy Spirit to work through you and give you spiritual eyes. STOP looking at scripture with your human mindset. If we could see the Bible through God's eyes, oh, what a different experience it would be!

When reading God's word you must begin to allow the Holy Spirit to work through you and give you spiritual eyes

Jesus is using metaphors in this passage to describe the spiritual realm we are fighting on a daily basis and the truths in His Word that He, God is our divine protection from the destruction of darkness.

The God of peace will soon crush satan under your feet. The grace of our Lord Jesus be with you. Romans 16:20 NIV

Jesus is NOT giving you instructions to physically handle deadly snakes to prove that His Power is displayed through you. The symbolism here is that there is a powerful and deadly enemy, satan, the serpent, who will not be able to stop God's mission or the success of it.

> Do not allow satan to misconstrue the meaning of God's word in order to keep you sidetracked

Do not allow satan to misconstrue the meaning of God's Word in order to keep you sidetracked from understanding how to use your Christ given authority.

There is only ONE constant and unchanging way by which demons are cast out and that is through the NAME OF JESUS!

The Name of Jesus is exalted above every other name.

Therefore God exalted Him to the highest place and gave Him the Name that is above every name, that at the Name of Jesus every knee should bow, in heaven and on earth and under the earth, and every tongue acknowledge that Jesus Christ is Lord, to the glory of God the Father. Philippians 2:9-11 NIV

It is the NAME of God.

It is the NAME that saves us.

It is the NAME that brings power to your authority in Christ.

Even demons know that!

> Demons will obey you when they know you understand your authority in Christ

Demons will obey you when they know you understand your authority in Christ and that you have dominion over them. When you use your Christ given authority you are representing Jesus. In other words, you are saying, "Jesus wants you out!"

God is a God of order and just like humans every being exits in order. Demons are no exception. They follow an order; the law that has been laid down in the courts of Heaven. Because you have active sin in your life you are agreeing with your addictive behaviors whether you realize it or not. Therefore, demons have legal right to stay. I have seen people cast demons out of themselves or someone else and then still manifest addictive behaviors.

> As a believer we have all authority to cast out demons in Jesus Name and they must obey

As a believer we have ALL Authority to cast out demons in Jesus Name and they must obey. HOWEVER, if you have not repented of the sins/addictive behaviors that allowed demons access in the first place they do not have to leave yet.

> if you want to get rid of addiction you have to repent

YET. That is the key word.

If you cast demons out with active sin still in your life you basically give them an eviction notice for an appointed time in the future. Their deadline to leave does not certify itself until you repent.

If you want to get rid of addiction you have to repent. When you ask forgiveness for the sinful nature of addiction you come out of agreement with the demon. Once the demon has no legal right to stay then by order it has to leave.

The power behind addiction is destroyed when you expel the demon(s) attached to the addictive behaviors.

It is time to CAST THEM OUT!

How Do I Cast Out Demons?

Demons come out by the power and anointing which only comes from the Holy Spirit. Your authority comes from Jesus, but the Power to cast out demons comes from the Holy Spirit.

> Demons come out by the power and anointing which only comes from the Holy Spirit

Jesus says, "But if I cast out demons by the Spirit of God, surely the Kingdom of God has come upon you." Matthew 12:28 NIV

"The Spirit of the Lord is upon Me, because He has anointed Me to preach the gospel to the poor; He has sent Me to heal the brokenhearted, to proclaim liberty to the

captives and recovery of sight to the blind, to set at liberty those who are oppressed." Luke 4:18 NIV

As a believer you need to cultivate awareness and intimacy dependent on Him. The most important being in casting out demons is the Holy Spirit.

Demons are NOT removed by going through therapy.

Demons are NOT removed by the confessing of sins.

Demons are NOT removed with a plea.

Yes. The flesh needs to be crucified.

Yes. You need repentance of sins,

and yes, you can plea bargain with the world, but demons need to be cast out.

You don't get demons by accident and you don't get them out with force. You have to want them out.

When Jesus arrived, demons manifested through people, but they did not leave just upon meeting Him. It wasn't until He cast them out, that they left.

> You don't get demons by accident and you don't get them out by force

Just then there was a man in their synagogue with an unclean spirit; and he cried out, saying,

"What business do we have with each other, Jesus of Nazareth? Have You come to destroy us? I know who You are, the Holy One of God! And Jesus rebuked him, saying, "Be quiet, and come out of him!" Throwing him into convulsions, the unclean spirit cried out with a loud vice and came out of him. They were all amazed, so that they debated among themselves, saying, what is this? A new teaching with authority! He commands even the unclean spirits, and they obey Him. Mark 1:23-27 AMP

Do not be misled by those who tell you that when you come to the altar, give your life to Jesus, and be born again that all your addictive behaviors, demons and curses will disappear. Yes, when you get born again you are a new creation in Christ Jesus and your name gets written down in the book of Life. However, demons don't leave just because you got saved. Again, you have to want them out.

Jesus did not force deliverance on anyone, neither did He go around casting demons out of everyone who had them.

I know that everyone's situation is not the same. I personally know people, including myself that when they sought Jesus, repented of their addictions and asked for deliverance they were never bothered again. They had no further compulsive impulses that accompany addiction.

When you seek refuge from the world instead of God's word alone you are further imprisoning yourself

While there are others who struggle with addictive behaviors in some form or another repeatedly. There are many different components involved in any single person's life that allow addictive behaviors to remain. Unrepentance, generational curses, open doors, multiple spirits and so forth. If you perpetually give in to the desires of addiction, there is a high likelihood you have opened up a doorway to the demonic realm. You are already in bondage from your addictions. When you seek refuge from the world instead of God's Word alone you are further imprisoning yourself. That is why it is so important to be infilled with the Holy Spirit and seek unity with Him always. In order to be effective you will need to always be walking in the Spirit. You can have Jesus as your authority, but without the Holy Spirit present you are powerless. Demons will easily overpower you, and vice versa. You can have the Holy Spirit and not the authority of Jesus and still be ineffective. Listen to the Holy Spirit and He will provide the revelation needed. Be obedient to what Jesus has called you to do and you will be able to drive them out.

Drive them out just as Jesus did.

That evening they brought to Him any who were oppressed by demons, and He cast out the spirits with a Word and healed all who were sick. Matthew 8:16 ESV

And He called to Him His twelve disciples and gave them authority over unclean spirits, to cast them out, and to heal every disease and every affliction. Matthew 10:1 ESV

"Heal the sick, raise the dead, cleanse those who have leprosy, drive out demons. Freely you have received; freely give." Matthew 10:8 NIV

And Jesus healed many who had various diseases. He also drove out many demons, but He would not let the demons speak because they knew who He was. Mark 1:34 NIV

And He went throughout all Galilee, preaching in their synagogues and casting out demons. Mark 1:39 ESV

There is no formula other than the NAME OF JESUS for casting out demons. Do not get wrapped up in there being a specific way to expel them. Religious

There is no formula other than the name of Jesus for casting out demons leaders are always looking for the right things to say. Witches and warlocks have certain incantations and spells they are required to cast. That is NOT biblical deliverance through the Holy Spirit.

There is NO repetition of specific words.

There is NO formula.

There are NO steps!

You must rely on the Holy Spirit alone to reveal to YOU which demons you are dealing with. Just like you and I, demons have names. Rely on the Holy Spirit and He will teach you all things.

"But the Helper, the Holy Spirit, whom the Father will send in My Name, He will teach you all things, and bring to your remembrance all things that I said to you." John 14:26 ESV

You do not have to wait until your next church service or revival to be free from your demons. You can cast them out with the help of the Holy Spirit right where you are.

You can even cast them out right now!

The first action calls for repentance

The first action calls for repentance. REPENT. Start by asking the Heavenly Father to forgive you of all active sin in your life including all addictive behaviors. I encourage you to even go one step further and accompany that repentance with actions. Throw away or cut out of your life everything that has contributed to your addictive behaviors. Whether that be friends, partners, drugs, alcohol, cigarettes, vape pens, junk food, pornography, sex or occultic items.

CUT THEM OFF in order to see lasting results.

RENOUNCE the curse of sin and break addictions over your life! As mentioned earlier, demons will hide in your physical body and your soul (mind and emotions).

Renounce the curse of sin and break addictions over your life

Say it OUTLOUD :

Holy Spirit, thank You for Your Power to heal and deliver. I know Your Word says all beings must bow before Your Name. Your Name is the Name above all names. There is none before You or after You. Thank You, Jesus for Your Blood. Thank You, Lord for Your revelation Power. I ask now in the Name of Jesus to break and release from me all generational curses and sins of my ancestors all the way back to Adam.

I break and release all curses of addiction, anger, pride, and rebellion ***(say anything else that the Holy Spirit brings to mind here)*** *over my life in the Name of Jesus.*

I break and release myself from all curses of death, premature death, murder, suicide, and destruction in the Name of Jesus.

I break and rebuke all curses of sickness, disease, and infirmity in the Name of Jesus.

I break and release from myself all curses of rejection, abandonment, and unworthiness in the Name of Jesus.

Any curses of mental illness, double-mindedness, and confusion I break and release now over me in the Name of Jesus.

Any curses of lust, perversion, molestation, sexual abuse, sodomy, I break you now in the Name of Jesus. Release me and go back to the pit in the Name of Jesus right now.

I break and release myself from all spoken curses, from all negative words spoken against me by others and by those in authority in Jesus Name. I, in turn bless my enemies and love all those who seek me harm.

I break and release myself from all self-inflicted curses by negative words I have spoken knowingly or unknowingly in the Name of Jesus.

Oh, Lord Jehovah hear my cry and rescue me from my afflicters. I praise You Alone, Jehovah Rapha for your healing Power in the Name of Jesus. You are God Almighty. Amen and Amen.

It is time to experience true freedom from your addictions in Jesus Name. Ask the Holy Spirit to reveal to you the names of demons present within and the areas they are operating in. As you go through this process you may experience some physical manifestations of the demons as they are being cast out. Symptoms like yawning, vomiting, body ticks, burping or ear popping are some of the things you might encounter. You are not alone. Trust the Holy Spirit to guide and help you throughout the deliverance. Most importantly, use the Authority given to you in Christ Jesus to speak LOUDLY and BOLDLY.

It is time to experience true freedom from your addictions in Jesus Name

Cast those demons out!

By the authority given to me through the Blood of Jesus I command every demon hiding and operating behind a curse to come out of me in the Name of Jesus. I am canceling your authority. You no longer have any legal right in my body or soul to be here. I cast you out! Leave in the

Name of Jesus. Go straight back to the abyss where you can harm no human no more.

Every demon of addiction, compulsiveness, addictive behaviors, anxiety, rejection, fear, torment (say other afflictions here as the Holy Spirit brings them to you), every demon coming from the bloodline of oaths and contracts, I break you now in the Name of Jesus. I cast you out now in Jesus Name. Return to the abyss and take all your seeds and filth with you in the Name of Jesus. Amen.

Inner Healing

I believe inner healing and deliverance (casting out of demons) are intertwined. In other words, to be healed is to be delivered and to be delivered is to be healed.

To be healed is to be delivered and to be delivered is to be healed

In order to experience complete freedom both need to be addressed.

How God anointed Jesus of Nazareth with the Holy Spirit and with power who went about doing good and healing all who were oppressed by the devil for God was with Him. Acts 10:38 NKJV

Inner healing is the healing that takes place inside of you. The deepest parts of your soul. Its main focus is on healing the soul realm which is your mind and emotions.

His Word Says…

"The Spirit of the Lord God is upon me, because the Lord has anointed Me to preach good tidings to the poor; He has sent Me to heal the brokenhearted, to proclaim liberty to the captives, and the opening of the prison to those who are bound;" Isaiah 61:1 NKJV

God instructs us to do three things:

Preach the gospel.

Heal the brokenhearted (inner healing)

Set the captives free (deliverance-to cast out demons).

Do you remember at the start of this book we talked about addictions initially being created from pain and trauma amongst other things? Here is where it all ties in.

Inner healing allows you to identify the deepest root of the trauma, and heal it permanently. It is not deliverance. However, it does involve casting out demons. Demonization is secondary to your inner hurt. Breaking curses and casting out demons in most cases will only

> Inner healing allows you to identify the deepest root of trauma, and heal it permanently

fix half of the problem. If you want to get rid of the demons attached to the wounds that birthed the addiction you have to remove all the hurt. You can cast out demons, but if the inner hurt remains they will return. This is why inner healing is so important. It is the elimination of all the leftover wounds, trauma, pain, and unresolved issues of your heart and soul.

When we experience trauma or anything that is too much for our souls to cope with, we disassociate. The world will tell you that disassociation is a mental illness. In all actuality it is a gift from God. It allows you to go away in your mind while the trauma or pain is taking place so you can survive. This disassociation creates a split or file in the back of the mind that holds all the pain and memory thereof. The severe trauma and abuse which often times occurs first during childhood is what causes these deep soul fractions. In consequence, these splits go unhealed and undealt with. Demons, including the demons of addiction are then allowed to come into that wound and sit on top of it creating torment. They create compulsive, uncontrollable behaviors.

Isn't that what addiction is?

> **If you want to heal from the inside out you need to be honest with yourself about your feelings**

If you want to continue to heal from the inside out you will need to be honest with yourself about your feelings and personal experiences. If you want the process of inner healing to work you have to come face to face with the emotion you felt in the moment.

Do you always tear up or have fresh feelings whenever you think about certain people or events that happened a long time ago in your past?

When someone says or does something you don't like do you immediately have intense feelings or a strong over reaction?

Do you ever wonder why you keep repeating the same negative situations or events?

If you said yes to any of these questions you probably have an unhealed wound.

Pay careful attention to your emotions.

When you have an elevated response observe your surroundings.

Become aware of the events that triggered the emotion. If you determine that you are overreacting there is a wound that needs to be healed.

Take all your hurts to Jesus and seek His Healing. Ask God to show you where it all started, and dig up the root of your addictive behaviors.

Take all your hurts to Jesus and seek his healing

God's Word has the healing power in it that you need. Have you ever heard anyone refer to the Bible as the "living" Word. It is just that: God's WORD. It was written by His very breath upon people He inspired to record His very heart and mind. The Holy Bible is NOT a natural book. It is infused by the very nature and presence of the Holy Spirit.

God's word has the healing power in it that you need

The holy bible is not a natural book

He sent His Word and healed them and delivered them from their destructions. Psalm 107:20 NKJV

Inner healing takes place by using prayer and God's Word to close those soul wounds. Seek His Word and let it speak to you.

Take as much time as you need.

Be quiet and still before the Lord.

Look and listen for Jesus, paying attention to any images, thoughts, or feelings that He may bring to your awareness.

God is our refuge and strength, a very present help in trouble.

Therefore we will not fear though the earth gives way, though the mountains be moved into the heart of the sea,

Though its waters roar and foam, though the mountains tremble at its swelling. Selah

There is a river whose streams make glad the city of God,

The holy habitation of the Most High. God is in the midst of her; she shall not be moved;

God will help her when morning dawns. The nations rage; the kingdoms totter; He utter His voice, the earth melts.

The Lord of hosts is with us; the God of Jacob is our fortress. Selah.

Come, behold the works of the Lord, how He has brought desolations on the earth; He breaks the bow and shatters the spear; He burns the chariots with fire.

"Be still, and know that I am God. I will be exalted among the nations, I will be exalted in the earth!"

Be still and know that He is God

The Lord of hosts is with us; the God of Jacob is our fortress. Selah. Psalm 46 NKJV

Be still and know that He is God.

Jesus will come. He will lay hold of the emotion and remove it by bringing truth to satan's lie. All you have to do is ask.

"Jesus, please come and heal this part of me."

After the wound is healed, tell all the demons on that wound to go to the pit, "In Jesus Name."

Now let God have control. You will reach that place of complete healing when you put your absolute trust in the Blood of Jesus. As you continue to give Him sovereignty, He will lead you into freedom.

Now let God have control

Declare Your Freedom

I will walk in freedom, for I have devoted myself to Your commandments. Psalm 119:45 NLT

Those who find Christ, the One and only source of spiritual truth, will be truly free. Devote yourself to God's Word and allow the Holy Spirit to direct your life.

> Devote yourself to God's Word and allow the Holy Spirit to direct your life

You are free, but you must continue to walk in that freedom. satan craves nothing more than to steal your joy.

Be sober minded; be watchful. Your adversary the devil prowls around like a roaring lion, seeking someone to devour. I Peter 5:8 ESV

The enemies of darkness are very aware they have lost the battle of addiction over your life. They will not hesitate to bring every demon of temptation to harass you. Their ultimate goal is to coax you into succumbing. Rebuke the devil and stay in God's Word.

Rebuke the devil and stay in God's word

Submit yourselves therefore to God. Resist the devil, and he will flee from you. James 4:7 KJV

In conclusion, stand on your deliverance and healing. Declare victory over yourself as you continue to strengthen in God's Word. Freedom is now yours!

Stand on your deliverance and healing

Verse:

He has delivered us from the power of darkness and conveyed us into the kingdom of the Son of His love, in whom we have redemption through His blood, the forgiveness of sins. Colossians 1:13-14

Proclamation:

I have been delivered from satan and now belong to the kingdom of God. I am redeemed by the Blood of Jesus, and since His blood was shed for me, I am completely forgiven of all my sins.

Verse:

But God demonstrates His own love toward us, in that while we were yet sinners, Christ dies for us. Much more then, having now been justified by His Blood, we shall be saved from wrath through Him. For if when we were enemies we were reconciled to God through the death of his Son, much more, having been reconciled, we shall be saved by His life. Romans 5:8-10 NIV

Proclamation:

I am loved unconditionally and perfectly by God and have been reconciled to Him through Christ's death. Jesus died in my place. His Blood covers me, therefore, when God looks at me He declares me righteous. I am free from all guilt, shame, and condemnation. "There is no condemnation in Christ Jesus."

Verse:
Christ has redeemed us from the curse of the law, having become a curse for us, that the blessing of Abraham might come upon the Gentiles in Christ Jesus, that we might receive the promise of the Spirit through faith. Galatians 3:13-14

Proclamation:
I am set free from every curse because Jesus became a curse for me on the cross. I have been redeemed by Christ. I am blessed and will walk in all the blessings that God has for me. I receive the Holy Spirit and will walk in His power.

Verse:
For the purpose of the Son of God was manifested, that He might destroy the works of the devil. I John 3:8

Proclamation:
The God of all peace crushes satan under my feet. Jesus came to destroy the works of darkness, and I declare that every work of the devil is destroyed in my life.

Verse:

"Behold, I give you the authority to trample on serpents and scorpion, and over all the power of the enemy, and nothing shall by any means hurt you. Nevertheless do not rejoice in this, that the spirits are subject to you, but rather rejoice because your names are written in heaven." Luke 10:19-20

Proclamation:

I trample on ALL the works of the devil because of the finished work of Jesus. In the Name of Jesus I have authority over every demon. I rejoice that my name is written in heaven, that I belong to God and am His child.

Verse:

God has not given us a spirit of fear, but of power and of love and of a sound mind. 2 Timothy 1:7

Proclamation:

God's perfect love casts out all fear. I am not subject to the spirit of fear, anxiety, or intimidation. He has filled me with the love and power of the Holy Spirit. My mind is clear, sound, and at peace. God's peace protects me even when I don't understand my circumstances.

Verse:

I will both lie down in peace, and sleep; for You alone, O Lord, make me dwell in safety. Psalm 4:8

Proclamation:

I declare that I will have peace in the night. My sleep belongs to the Lord. He gives me rest and comfort.

Verse:

Therefore, if anyone is in Christ, he is a new creation; old things have passed away; behold, all things have become new. 2 Corinthians 5:17

Proclamation:

I am a new creation in Christ. I am identified by His death, resurrection, and ascension I will not be defined by my past nor held back in my destiny. By the Blood of Jesus I am free.

Conclusion

When I was a child and growing up into adolescence I saw and heard things I could not explain in the natural world. I did not understand back then what I know now, and had no one to teach me about my Christ identity. In turn, I was repeatedly told there must be something wrong with me. After a while I began to believe that lie, and a wound was created. Through the years, I began to look for love in all the wrong places. I wanted to be accepted for who I thought I was. Eventually I turned to drugs and alcohol to make the rejection I felt inside go away. In consequence, I married someone with the demons of addiction, and became stuck in a cycle of abuse for twenty more years. It wasn't really until after that time I began to learn God loved me for me, and that His love alone was all I would ever need. He created me for a unique purpose. It took many years to discover the Holy Spirit's function in my life, the importance of knowing my Christ identity, and how to wade through the process of inner healing in order to obtain true freedom. That is why my burning devotion to share the knowledge I have grasped through my relationship with the Holy Spirit is so strong. He is my very best friend, and now that I have found Him I could not imagine what my life was ever like before Him. I do not want anyone to wait as long as I did before they understand these truths in God's Word. My passion is for everyone to know Christ and obtain the complete, whole, and true freedom available through the Power of His Name and the Blood of Jesus that made it all possible. My utmost desire and the desire of Mended Heart is to see people healed, strengthened and restored through Jesus. My prayer for you is that you take the knowledge throughout these pages and seek the Holy Spirit with every fiber of your being. Seek Him until you find Him, and never let go.

Copper B.

Psalm 63

O God, You are my God; earnestly I seek You;
my soul thirsts for You;
my flesh faints for You,
as in a dry and weary land where there is no water.
2 *So I have looked upon You in the sanctuary,*
beholding Your power and glory.
3 *Because Your steadfast love is better than life,*
my lips will praise You.
4 *So I will bless You as long as I live;*
in Your name I will lift up my hands.
5 *My soul will be satisfied as with fat and rich food,*
and my mouth will praise You with joyful lips,
6 *when I remember You upon my bed,*
and meditate on You in the watches of the night;
7 *for You have been my help,*
and in the shadow of Your wings I will sing for joy.
8 *My soul clings to You;*
Your right hand upholds me.
9 *But those who seek to destroy my life*
shall go down into the depths of the earth;
10 *they shall be given over to the power of the sword;*
they shall be a portion for jackals.
11 *But the king shall rejoice in God;*
all who swear by Him shall exult,
for the mouths of liars will be stopped.

Dangers of 12 Step Recovery Programs in Churches

When we first started in this journey of bringing the hope of Jesus to the broken hearted we became more deeply involved with addiction recovery as a resource to aid those searching for a way to heal and be free. What we soon discovered was that a lot of people in these programs seemed to still be recovering after a substantial amount of time. Years even. The more we heard recovery is a continual process and that the importance of the 12 steps is instrumental to the success of recovery, the more we started to question the root and effectiveness of these programs. Anyone who knows me on a personal level acknowledges that when I don't understand facts about a subject or I experience what I like to call my "silent alarm bell", I start to dig. That is what happened concerning the explosion surrounding these 12 step programs in churches. I started to delve a little deeper into their root system.

There are all kinds of step programs throughout the Evangelical church today. The 12 step recovery programs in particular knowing or unknowingly use man centered methods guised in scripture, yet rooted in darkness. satan is not called the father of lies for nothing.

Satan is not called the father of lies for nothing

You belong to your father, the devil, and you want to carry out your father's desires. He was a murderer from the beginning, not holding to the truth, for there is no truth in him. When he lies, he speaks his native language, for he is a liar and the father of all lies. John 8:44 NIV

The great dragon was hurled down, that ancient serpent called the devil, or satan, who leads the whole world astray. He was hurled to the earth, and his angels with him. Revelation 12:9 NIV

The history of the 12 step recovery programs in churches stems all the way back to the foundation of the secular Alcohol Anonymous (AA). The inspiration for AA ultimately came from a well-known psychiatrist named Carl Jung. Jung was noted for his spiritualist roots. He credited his great perception, wisdom and ideas for the 12 steps associated with AA to his consultation with his very own spirit guide- a religious spirit. Jung treated a patient named Roland Hazard who was so enthralled by his practices that he founded a religious organization called The Oxford Group. Out of that group came Bill Wilson who is the co-founder of Alcohol Anonymous. Wilson to this day credits Jung as being the true founder of AA because of the influence of his spiritual wisdom. In turn, the Christian 12 step movement originated out of the roots of the AA steps. This is where it begins to get dangerous for anyone whether a born again believer in Christ or someone who is unsaved. The only real difference between the secular 12 steps and the church program steps is that religious programs modified them in a way to add Jesus and use scripture as their basis. What they don't realize is that satan uses this Christian veneer displayed by these programs as a hidden disguise to deceive God's people. satan is not

> Satan uses the christian veneer displayed by these programs as a hidden disguise to deceive God's people

ignorant. He knows the more the teachings and ideas of these programs sounds like biblical Christian truth, the easier one will be led astray. You cannot take ANY doctrine rooted in the demonic realm, add Jesus to it, and turn it into something Biblical based. In short, you can NOT start with evil and repackage it as holy. IT WILL NOT WORK.

> You can not start with evil and repackage it as holy

Why?

Because the ROOT is still the same.

There is NOT a problem with recovery. There are many people who need extra help navigating some of life's devastating circumstances. There is nothing wrong with seeking out sound biblical counseling, a strong group of prayer partners, a Christ rooted recovery program or even medical attention.

> There is not a problem with recovery

The issue lies when the program bases itself in the ROOTS of religious practices that stem from a higher power that is NOT God, our Heavenly Father. The One and Only God Almighty.

This is where you have to be careful!

Some are unknowingly coming into these programs with a higher power other than God that is already attached to them. In consequence, when you call on that higher power as part of the program you are unintentionally speaking to a familiar spirit and not to God. You are then ultimately arriving at you instead of dying to self.

I have been crucified with Christ, it is no longer I who live, but Christ who lives in me. And the life I now live in the flesh I live by faith in the Son of God, who loved me and gave Himself for me. Galatians 2:20

And He said to all "if anyone would come after Me, let him deny himself and take up his cross daily and follow Me." Luke 9:23

And those who belong to Christ Jesus have crucified the flesh with its passions and desires. Galatians 5:24

Truly, truly, I say to you, unless a grain of wheat falls into the earth and dies, it remains alone; but if it dies, it bears much fruit. John 12:24

In addition, what about the people in these programs who are stuck. The ones who get stuck in the steps or addicted to the program.

Why does this happen?

Because the steps are NOT God. They use and reference God. In all actuality, when you rely on the 12 steps to better yourself you are unknowingly redefining God's plan of salvation, calling it recovery, and programming a doctrine. In turn, recovery and the steps accidentally take the place of Jesus and, consequently, form a works based religion. That's why you end up not only trading your addiction, but, in fact, you may still carry the one you originally started with as well.

The steps are not God

When you never search deep enough to dig up the root then addiction will always cycle back around to where? The root.

Is that not the culprit in all problem areas of our lives?

The ROOT?

When you uncover the root, the lie is exposed. Therefore, when you reveal addiction at its root you get rid of it for good. You don't need the 12 steps in order to arrive at a state of

When you uncover the root, the lie is exposed

being recovered. What you need is to start and end with Jesus.

Period.

Instead of using 12 step programs, whether or not created in demonic roots, start with the Word of God. Build your program on Jesus, the Holy Spirit, and scripture.

> The answer to healing and recovery is in the living word of God

The answer to healing and recovery is in the Living Word of God. That alone is all you need.

Do not get me wrong. I am not saying these programs have not helped people along the way. I am sure some individuals have even repented and become born again believers in Christ. There are others who went through Christian 12-step recovery, moved forward and never looked back. God can certainly use what man has put together to bring glory to His Name.

> When you are at your lowest point that is when Satan seeks to deceive you

What I AM saying is even if the program

you are involved in has Christian terminology to it, look closely at who is teaching it, who created it, and where the roots of it were established. When you are at your lowest point that is when satan seeks to deceive you. Lucifer comes as deception of light. His time is short and he knows it. That's why he wants nothing more than to keep as many as possible from following Christ and finding their God given purpose. Even if you are in God's Word and praying, when you are desperate to find answers it is easy to be led astray. If you have any doubt, go back to the Bible. Ground yourself in scripture, surround yourself with others rooted in sound Biblical doctrine, and seek the Holy Spirit.

If you have any doubt go back to the bible

It is our duty to share biblical knowledge

Our goal is not to cause conflict between ourselves and the people involved in these type programs in any way. Mended Heart Ministry services and serves with many individuals who attend, volunteer or teach in these programs. We love and deeply care about each and everyone. However, it is part of our duty in Christ

Jesus to share the Biblical knowledge we have learned along the way, and bring awareness to God's people.

We must help build one another up

Satan craves nothing more than to divide and deceive. That is why we must continually strive to push back and expose the secret works of darkness by helping build one another up in the ways of the Lord. If nothing else it is our genuine desire as a ministry to continually seek the very heart of God. Therefore, ultimately, we want to encourage you to build a relationship in Him, strengthen your walk in the Lord, and uncover the devil's tactics that keep you bound.

As iron sharpens iron, so one person sharpens another. Proverbs 27:17 NIV

Now, brothers and sisters, about times and dates we do not need to write to you, [2] for you know very well that the day of the Lord will come like a thief in the night.[3] While people are saying, "Peace and safety," destruction will come on them suddenly, as labor pains on a pregnant woman, and they will not escape.

[4]But you, brothers and sisters, are not in darkness so that this day should surprise you like a thief. [5] You are

all children of the light and children of the day. We do not belong to the night or to the darkness. [6] So then, let us not be like others, who are asleep, but let us be awake and sober. [7] For those who sleep, sleep at night, and those who get drunk, get drunk at night. [8] But since we belong to the day, let us be sober, putting on faith and love as a breastplate, and the hope of salvation as a helmet. [9] For God did not appoint us to suffer wrath but to receive salvation through our Lord Jesus Christ. [10] He died for us so that, whether we are awake or asleep, we may live together with him. [11] Therefore encourage one another and build each other up, just as in fact you are doing.

[12] Now we ask you, brothers and sisters, to acknowledge those who work hard among you, who care for you in the Lord and who admonish you. [13] Hold them in the highest regard in love because of their work. Live in peace with each other. [14] And we urge you, brothers and sisters, warn those who are idle and disruptive, encourage the disheartened, help the weak, be patient with everyone. [15] Make sure that nobody pays back wrong for wrong, but always strive to do what is good for each other and for everyone else.

[16] Rejoice always, [17] pray continually, [18] give thanks in all circumstances; for this is God's will for you in Christ Jesus.

**[19] Do not quench the Spirit. [20] Do not treat proph-
ecies with contempt [21] but test them all; hold on to
what is good, [22] reject every kind of evil.**

[23] May God himself, the God of peace, sanctify you
through and through. May your whole spirit, soul and
body be kept blameless at the coming of our Lord Jesus
Christ. [24] The one who calls you is faithful, and he will
do it.

[25] Brothers and sisters, pray for us. [26] Greet all God's
people with a holy kiss. [27] I charge you before the Lord
to have this letter read to all the brothers and sisters.

[28] The grace of our Lord Jesus Christ be with you. I
Thessalonians 5 NIV

Shalom Aleikhem

Who Am I Scripture References

Always remember your true identity is found in who Christ is. You are identified IN CHRIST. The moment you accept Him into your life as your Savior, you are HIS; adopted into the family of God.

Your true identity is found in who Christ is

I am His.

He brought me to the banqueting-house, And His banner over me was love. Solomon 2:4

I am bought with a price.

Now you are the body of Christ and individually members of it. I Cor. 12:27

I am a Child of God.

See what kind of love the Father has given to us, that we should be called children of God; and so *we are. The reason why the world does not know us is that it did not know him. I John 3:1*

I am a brand new creation.

Therefore, if anyone is in Christ, he is a new creation. The old has passed away; behold, the new has come. 2 Cor. 5:17

I am chosen.

But you are a chosen race, a royal priesthood, a holy nation, a people for his own possession, that you may proclaim the excellencies of Him who called you out of darkness into His marvelous light. I Peter 2:9

My life is in Christ.

I have been crucified with Christ. It is no longer I who live, but Christ who lives in me. And the life I now live in the flesh I live by faith in the Son of God, who loved me and gave Himself for me. Gal. 2:20

I am precious and honored.

Because you are precious in my eyes, and honored, and I love you, I give men in return for you, peoples in exchange for your life. Isaiah 43:4

I am an heir to God.

and if children, then heirs—heirs of God and fellow heirs with Christ, provided we suffer with Him in order that we may also be glorified with Him. Romans 8:17

I am completed in Christ Jesus.

and you have been filled in Him, who is the head of all rule and authority. Colossians 2:10

I am established and anointed by God.

And it is God who establishes us with you in Christ, and has anointed us, [22] and who has also put His seal on us and given us His Spirit in our hearts as a guarantee 2 Cor. 1:21-22

I am hidden in God.

For you have died, and your life is hidden with Christ in God. Colossians 3:3

I am God's temple.

Do you not know that you are God›s temple and that God›s Spirit dwells in you? I Corinthians 3:16

I am free from condemnation.

There is therefore now no condemnation for those who are in Christ Jesus. [2] For the law of the Spirit of life has set you free in Christ Jesus from the law of sin and death. Romans 8:1-2

I know all things work together for good.

And we know that for those who love God all things work together for good, for those who are called according to His purpose. Romans 8:28

I am free from any charge against me.

What then shall we say to these things? If God is for us, who can be against us? [32] He who did not spare his own Son but gave Him up for us all, how will He not also with Him graciously give us all things? [33] Who shall bring any charge against God's elect? It is God who justifies. [34] Who is to condemn? Christ Jesus is the One who died—more than that, who was raised—who is at the right Hand of God, who indeed is interceding for us. Romans 8:31-34

I have been adopted as God's child..

He predestined us for adoption to Himself as sons through Jesus Christ, according to the purpose of His will, Ephesians 1:5

I have been justified.

Therefore, since we have been justified by faith, we have peace with God through our Lord Jesus Christ. Romans 5:1

I may approach God with freedom and confidence.

in whom we have boldness and access with confidence through our faith in Him. Ephesians 3:12

I have access to God through the Holy Spirit.

For through Him we both have access in one Spirit to the Father. Ephesians 2:18

I have been redeemed.

in whom we have redemption, the forgiveness of sins. Colossians 1:14

I can do all things through Christ.

I can do all things through Him who strengthens me. Philippians 4:13

Sample Prayers

Repentance Prayer

Nothing hinders your prayer life more than unconfessed sin. You need to get real with God. There is no better way to do that than repentance.

Dear Heavenly Father, thank You for Your promise of forgiveness that I may come to the cross for cleansing. There is no greater grace than this. Thank You, Lord for giving me a fresh awareness of my sin so that I can bring it before You, the Almighty God. Forgive me, Father for the things in my life that are not pleasing to You. As David said in his Psalm:

Have mercy on me, O God,
according to your unfailing love;
according to your great compassion
blot out my transgressions.

**2Wash away all my iniquity
and cleanse me from my sin.
3For I know my transgressions,
and my sin is always before me.
4Against you, you only, have I sinned
and done what is evil in your sight;
so you are right in your verdict
and justified when you judge.
5Surely I was sinful at birth,
sinful from the time my mother conceived me.
6Yet you desired faithfulness even in the womb;
you taught me wisdom in that secret place.
7Cleanse me with hyssop, and I will be clean;
wash me, and I will be whiter than snow.
8Let me hear joy and gladness;
let the bones you have crushed rejoice.
9Hide your face from my sins
and blot out all my iniquity.
10Create in me a pure heart, O God,
and renew a steadfast spirit within me.
11Do not cast me from your presence
or take your Holy Spirit from me.
12Restore to me the joy of your salvation
and grant me a willing spirit, to sustain me.
13Then I will teach transgressors your ways,
so that sinners will turn back to you.**

14Deliver me from the guilt of bloodshed, O God,
you who are God my Savior,
and my tongue will sing of your righteousness.
15Open my lips, Lord,
and my mouth will declare your praise.
16You do not delight in sacrifice, or I would bring it;
you do not take pleasure in burnt offerings.
17My sacrifice, O God, is a broken spirit;
a broken and contrite heart
you, God, will not despise.
18May it please you to prosper Zion,
to build up the walls of Jerusalem.
19Then you will delight in the sacrifices of the righteous,
in burnt offerings offered whole;
then bulls will be offered on your altar. Psalm 51

Trust in God Prayer

Even when you can't see it, God is fighting for you. He has a plan. Trust Him to get you there.

O Lord my God, El Shaddai, help me to trust in what is unseen. Thank You that You are my help in time of trouble. Remind me, Lord of Your truth and Your Power. Surround me with Your might. I praise You as You continue to fight me. You are the King of Kings, the Only God. All glory and honor be forever and ever to You. Amen.

Breakthrough Prayer

Breakthrough happens when you take that first step and trust God to do the impossible in your life.

Faithful God, thank You for being the Resurrection and the Life. The Power that You used to conquer death now lives in me. Lord, I pray that I understand Your all-conquering power in my life today and experience a breakthrough. At Your Name mountains shake. At Your Name every knee will bow and every tongue confess that You are Lord. At Your Name demons flee. Work Your Power in my life, Almighty Father. In Jesus Name. Amen.

Meet My Needs Prayer

God will meet you right where you are. Never doubt He can't supply your every need. You just have to ask.

Loving Father, thank You for loving me. Thank You, Lord that all things were created by You in heaven as well as earth. You have promised those that seek You shall find You and lack no good thing. I pray, Lord let me look to You for every need and desire in my life. Pour out Your blessings upon me. Show me Your love. May I see Your beauty in everything. Thank You, Jesus. Amen.

Mental Healing Prayer

The Lord is close to the brokenhearted and saves those who are crushed in spirit. Psalm 34:18

Jesus, I am feeling the strain of this world as I am walking in hard places. My mind is struggling and I can't seem to cope. Lord, Jesus I ask You to come beside me now. Lead me through this time of mental anguish. Help me to find peace and calm my inner thoughts. Lord God I trust in You and You alone. In the Name of Jesus, fill me with Your presence. Holy Spirit burn like a fire through me so there is nothing left of me. Only You. In the Name of Jesus. Amen

Fear, Doubt and Anxiety Prayer

The Lord says in His Word, He will never leave nor forsake you. He wants you to bring all your fears and worries and lay them at His feet. He will carry them for you.

Lord God, I know in Your Word You say, "Do not be anxious about anything, but in everything by prayer and supplication with thanksgiving let my requests be made known unto You." So, Lord, I come before You now. I am laying all my fear and anxiety at Your feet. Help me , Lord. Remind me that You are all Powerful. I rebuke, fear, in the Name of Jesus it has no place in my life. Help me to keep my eyes on You, Heavenly Father. Always. In the matchless name of Jesus I ask these things now . Amen and Amen.

Peace Prayer

God is our Prince of Peace.

Abba, Father, I come before You pouring out my heart. All my worries I bring to Your feet. I am declaring Your promises for blessings and peace over my life, Lord Jesus. Bring peace into my soul that passes all worldy understanding. My desire, O God, is that You make me a light of peace for others to see. Amen.

Endurance Prayer

In the most difficult times of your life rely on God to sustain you. By keeping your faith strong you will be able to get through trials without compromising or wavering.

Heavenly Father, You have said in Your Word that I need not to be afraid to go through hard times. Instead, I should be thankful for the gift of endurance. Lord Jesus, You have always been faithful to me. I ask You, now that in the darkness of discouragement, give me the light of Your Presence. Help me to endure to the end. Thank You, Almighty God for You are worthy of all things. Amen

Prayer to Strengthen Faith

Boldy go before the Father and ask for more faith. Ask for strengthened faith that will grow your trust and confidence in what is true. Not what is seen, but what is unseen.

Lord, thank You for Your infinite mercy and grace. You are the Maker of all, and hold all things in the palm of Your hand. Lord, I come to You now asking You to increase my faith and make me a mover of mountains. Grow my belief in You alone so that I can be strong in You and ready to battle any doubt planted by the enemy. Thank You, Abba Father. Amen.

Prayer for Resisting the Devil

Whenever you feel tempted, resist the devil and draw closer to God. Be bold, and put on His full armor!

God, the Mighty Warrior, thank you so much for always protecting me in all areas of my life. I ask You, Father to bless me today with the strength I need to resist the devil and all spiritual attacks the enemy will send my way. Draw me closer to You, Lord. God Almighty, Bless and strengthen me, Lord as I put on the full armor of God. With Your helmet of salvation I block out from my mind all evil lies. I firmly cinch shut the breastplate of righteousness as I fasten the belt of truth across my groin. Give me the strength even now, O God, to raise up my shield of faith as You defend me against all the flaming darts of the enemy. Lord, arm me with the sword of the Spirit, Your Holy Bible. Lastly, I strap by boots of peace, so that I can turn to You in all that I do and trust in You, Lord for faith and courage. Thank You, Jesus. Amen.

Scripture Glossary

Ephesians 6:12 NIV
For our struggle is not against flesh and blood, but against the rulers, against the authorities, against the powers of this dark world and against the spiritual forces of evil in the heavenly realms.

Ecclesiastes 3:11 AMP
He has made everything beautiful *and* appropriate in its time. He has also planted eternity [a sense of divine purpose] in the human heart [a mysterious longing which nothing under the sun can satisfy, except God]—yet man cannot find out (comprehend, grasp) what God has done (His overall plan) from the beginning to the end.

Genesis 1:27 NKJV
So God created mankind in His own image, in the image of God He created them; male and female He created them.

John 4:24 NKJV
God *is* Spirit, and those who worship Him must worship in spirit and truth.

Genesis 2:7 NIV
And the LORD God formed man *of* the dust of the ground, and breathed into his nostrils the breath of life; and man became a living being.

Ecclesiastes 12:7 NKJV
Then the dust will return to the earth as it was,
And the spirit will return to God who gave it.

Hebrews 4:12 NIV
For the word of God is alive and active. Sharper than any double-edged sword, it penetrates even to dividing soul and spirit, joints and marrow; it judges the thoughts and attitudes of the heart.

Acts 10:38 NLT
And you know that God anointed Jesus of Nazareth with the Holy Spirit and with power. Then Jesus went around doing good and healing all who were oppressed by the devil, for God was with Him.

I Corinthians 3:16-17 ESV
Do you not know that you are God's temple and that
God's Spirit dwells in you? 17 If anyone destroys God's
temple, God will destroy him. For God's temple is holy,
and you are that temple.

John 10:29 ESV
My Father, who has given them to me, is greater than all, and no one is able to snatch them out of the Father's Hand.

2 Thessalonians 2:8 NLT
Then the man of lawlessness will be revealed, but the Lord Jesus will slay him with the breath of His mouth and destroy him by the splendor of His coming.

Revelation 1:8 NKJV
I am the Alpha and the Omega, *the* Beginning and *the* End," says the Lord, "who is and who was and who is to come, the Almighty."

Exodus 3:12 NKJV
So He said, "I will certainly be with you. And this *shall be* a sign to you that I have sent you: When you have brought the people out of Egypt, you shall serve God on this mountain."

James 33:3 AMP
"Call to Me and I will answer you, and tell you (and even show you) great and mighty things, (things which have been confined and hidden), which you do not know and understand and cannot distinguish."

Ephesians 2:10 NLT
For we are God's masterpiece. He has created us anew in Christ Jesus, so we can do the good things he planned for us long ago.

Romans 8:38-39 NKJV
For I am persuaded that neither death nor life, nor angels nor principalities nor powers, nor things present nor things to come, [39] nor height nor depth, nor any other created thing, shall be able to separate us from the love of God which is in Christ Jesus our Lord.

John 15:19 NIV
If you belonged to the world, it would love you as its own. As it is, you do not belong to the world, but I have chosen you out of the world. That is why the world hates you.

Mark 8:34 NIV
Then he called the crowd to Him along with His disciples and said: "Whoever wants to be my disciple must deny themselves and take up their cross and follow me."

Matthew 6:33 NIV
But seek first His kingdom and His righteousness, and all these things will be given to you as well.

John 3:16 KJV
For God so loved the world that He gave His only begotten Son, that whosoever believeth in Him should not perish but have everlasting life.

Jeremiah 29:11-13 NIV
For I know the plans I have for you," declares the LORD,
"plans to prosper you and not to harm you, plans to give
you hope and a future. [12]Then you will call on Me and
come and pray to Me, and I will listen to you. [13]You will
seek Me and find Me when you seek Me with all your
heart.

Psalm 119:11 NIV
I have hidden Your word in my heart that I might not sin against You.

Proverbs 18:21 NLT
The tongue can bring death or life; those who love to talk will reap the consequences.

Proverbs 15:4 NIV
The soothing tongue is a tree of life, but a perverse tongue crushes the spirit.

Proverbs 12:18 BST
Speaking rashly is like a piercing sword, but the tongue of the wise brings healing.

James 3:9 NLT
With the tongue we praise our Lord and Father, and with it we curse human beings, who have been made in God's likeness.

Isaiah 53:5 NKJV
But He *was* wounded for our transgressions,
He was bruised for our iniquities;
The chastisement for our peace *was* upon Him,
And by His stripes we are healed.

John 10:10 NIV
The thief comes only to steal and kill and destroy; I have come that they may have life, and have it to the full.

2 Corinthians 10:3-4 NIV
For though we live in the world, we do not wage war as
the world does. [4]The weapons we fight with are not the
weapons of the world. On the contrary, they have divine
power to demolish strongholds.

John 20:21-22 NIV
Again Jesus said, "Peace be with you! As the Father
has sent Me, I am sending you." [22]And with that He
breathed on them and said, "Receive the Holy Spirit."

Acts 8:16-18 NLT
The Holy Spirit had not yet come upon any of them, for
they had only been baptized in the Name of the Lord
Jesus. [17]Then Peter and John laid their hands upon these
believers, and they received the Holy Spirit.

Acts 19:1-7 NKJV
And it happened, while Apollos was at Corinth, that
Paul, having passed through the upper regions, came to
Ephesus. And finding some disciples [2]he said to them,
"Did you receive the Holy Spirit when you believed?"

So they said to him, "We have not so much as heard
whether there is a Holy Spirit."

3 And he said to them, "Into what then were you
baptized?"

So they said, "Into John's baptism."

4 Then Paul said, "John indeed baptized with a baptism
of repentance, saying to the people that they should
believe on Him who would come after him, that is, on
Christ Jesus."

5 When they heard *this,* they were baptized in the name
of the Lord Jesus. 6 And when Paul had laid hands on
them, the Holy Spirit came upon them, and they spoke
with tongues and prophesied. 7 Now the men were
about twelve in all.

Acts 1:4-5 NKJV
And being assembled together with *them,* He commanded them not to depart from Jerusalem, but to wait
for the Promise of the Father, "which," *He said,* "you
have heard from Me; 5 for John truly baptized with
water, but you shall be baptized with the Holy Spirit
not many days from now."

Luke 24:49 NLT
"And now I will send the Holy Spirit, just as my Father promised. But stay here in the city until the Holy Spirit comes and fills you with power from heaven."

Acts 1:8 ESV

But you will receive power when the Holy Spirit has come upon you, and you will be my witnesses in Jerusalem and in all Judea and Samaria, and to the end of the earth."

Joel 2:28-29 NKJV

"And it shall come to pass afterward
That I will pour out My Spirit on all flesh;
Your sons and your daughters shall prophesy,
Your old men shall dream dreams,
Your young men shall see visions.
29 And also on *My* menservants and on *My* maidser-
vants I will pour out My Spirit in those days.

Luke 11:13 NKJV

If you then, being evil, know how to give good gifts to your children, how much more will *your* heavenly Father give the Holy Spirit to those who ask Him!"

Matthew 7:7 ESV

"Ask, and it will be given to you; seek, and you will find; knock, and it will be opened to you."

Luke 11:10 NKJV
For everyone who asks receives, and he who seeks finds, and to him who knocks it will be opened.

2 Corinthians 3:17 NIV
Now the Lord is the Spirit, and where the Spirit of the Lord is, there is freedom.

Luke 10:19 ESV
Behold, I have given you authority to tread on serpents and scorpions, and over all the power of the enemy, and nothing shall hurt you.

John 14:12 ESV
"Truly, truly, I say to you, whoever believes in me will also do the works that I do; and greater works than these will he do, because I am going to the Father.

Mark 16:17 NIV
And these signs will accompany those who believe: In my name they will drive out demons; they will speak in new tongues;

Matthew 10:7-8 NIV
As you go, proclaim this message: 'The kingdom of
heaven has come near.' 8 Heal the sick, raise the dead,

cleanse those who have leprosy,[a] drive out demons. Freely you have received; freely give.

I Peter 2:11 KJV
Dearly beloved, I beseech you as strangers and pilgrims, abstain from fleshly lusts, which war against the soul;

Mark 16:17-20 NIV
And these signs will accompany those who believe: In
my name they will drive out demons; they will speak
in new tongues; 18 they will pick up snakes with their
hands; and when they drink deadly poison, it will not
hurt them at all; they will place their hands on sick people, and they will get well."
19 After the Lord Jesus had spoken to them, he was
taken up into heaven and he sat at the right hand of
God. 20 Then the disciples went out and preached every-
where, and the Lord worked with *them and confirmed his word by the signs that accompanied it.*

Romans 16:20 NIV
The God of peace will soon crush Satan under your feet. The grace of our Lord Jesus be with you.

Philippians 2:9-11 NIV
Therefore God exalted him to the highest place and gave him the name that is above every name, [10] that at the name of Jesus every knee should bow, in heaven and on earth and under the earth, [11] and every tongue acknowledge that Jesus Christ is Lord, to the glory of God the Father.

Matthew 12:28 NIV
But if it is by the Spirit of God that I drive out demons, then the kingdom of God has come upon you.

Luke 4:18 NIV
"The Spirit of the Lord is on Me,
  because He has anointed Me
  to proclaim good news to the poor.
He has sent Me to proclaim freedom for the prisoners
  and recovery of sight for the blind,
to set the oppressed free,"

Mark 1:23-27 AMP
Just then there was a man in their synagogue with an unclean spirit; and he cried out terribly from the depths of his throat, [24] saying, "What business do You have with us, Jesus of Nazareth? Have You come to destroy us?

I know who You are—the Holy One of God!" [25] Jesus
rebuked him, saying, "Be quiet (muzzled, silenced),
and come out of him!" [26] The unclean spirit threw the
man into convulsions, and screeching with a loud voice,
came out of him. [27] They were all so amazed that they
debated *and* questioned each other, saying, "What is
this? A new teaching with authority! He commands
even the unclean spirits (demons), and they obey Him."

Matthew 8:16 ESV
That evening they brought to him many who were oppressed by demons, and he cast out the spirits with a word and healed all who were sick.

Matthew 10:1 ESV
And he called to him his twelve disciples and gave them authority over unclean spirits, to cast them out, and to heal every disease and every affliction.

Matthew 10:8 NIV
Heal the sick, raise the dead, cleanse those who have leprosy, drive out demons. Freely you have received; freely give.

Matthew 1:34 NIV
And Jesus healed many who had various diseases. He also drove out many demons, but He would not let the demons speak because they knew who He was.

Mark 1:39 ESV
And He went throughout all Galilee, preaching in their synagogues and casting out demons.

John 14:26 ESV
But the Helper, the Holy Spirit, whom the Father will send in my name, he will teach you all things and bring to your remembrance all that I have said to you.

Isaiah 61:1 NKJV
"The Spirit of the Lord GOD *is* upon Me,
Because the LORD has anointed Me
To preach good tidings to the poor;
He has sent Me toheal the brokenhearted,
To proclaim liberty to the captives,
And the opening of the prison to *those who are* bound;

Psalm 107:20 NKJV
He sent His word and healed them,
And delivered *them* from their destructions.

Copper B.

Psalm 46 NKJV
God *is* our refuge and strength,
A very present help in trouble.
[2]Therefore we will not fear,
Even though the earth be removed,
And though the mountains be carried into the midst of the sea;
[3]*Though* its waters roar *and* be troubled,
Though the mountains shake with its swelling. *Selah*
[4]*There is* a river whose streams shall make glad the city of God,
The holy *place* of thetabernacle of the Most High.
[5]God *is* in the midst of her, she shall not be moved;
God shall help her, justat the break of dawn.
[6]The nations raged, the kingdoms were moved;
He uttered His voice, the earth melted.
[7]The LORD of hosts *is* with us;
The God of Jacob *is* our refuge. *Selah*
[8]Come, behold the works of the LORD,
Who has made desolations in the earth.
[9]He makes wars cease to the end of the earth;
He breaks the bow and cuts the spear in two;
He burns the chariot in the fire.
[10]Be still, and know that I *am* God;
I will be exalted among the nations,
I will be exalted in the earth!

[11] The LORD of hosts *is* with us;
The God of Jacob *is* our refuge. *Selah*

Psalm 119:45 NLT
I will walk in freedom,
for I have devoted myself to your commandments.

Peter 5:8 ESV
Be sober minded; be watchful. Your adversary the devil prowls around like a roaring lion, seeking someone to devour.

James 4:7 KJV
Submit yourselves therefore to God. Resist the devil, and he will flee from you.

Notes

After you have read this entire book, I encourage you to go back through the pages and jot down anything you don't understand, have questions about, or are further interested in learning. Begin to search the scriptures. Delve into God's Word and seek the answers for yourself. Allow the Holy Spirit to speak to you, and show you great and mighty things you do not know.

Hello My Name Is

Copper B.

Hello My Name Is

Copper B.

Hello My Name Is

Copper B.

Hello My Name Is

Made in the USA
Middletown, DE
14 May 2023

30097575R00085